PATTER

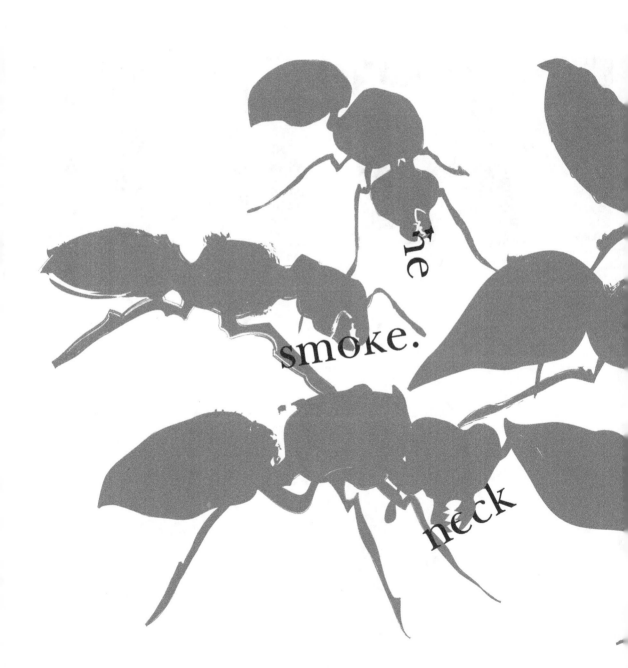

against

knocking

its

broken

first edition
published in the United States by
RED HEN PRESS | *Pasadena, CA*
www.redhen.org

10 9 8 7 6 5 4 3 2

TER

POEMS

DOUGLAS KEARNEY

set in Mendoza; display in Van Condensed | author photo by Eric Plattner | printed by
United Graphics Inc |
Library of Congress cataloguing-in-publication data | Kearney, Douglas,
1974– | [Poems. Selections] | Patter: poems / by Douglas Kearney.—First edition. |
p. cm. | ISBN 978-1-59709-580-8 (alk. Paper) | I. Title | PS3611.E177P382014 | 811'.6—dc23

For E, K, & N

. . .the night is beginning to lower. . .
I hear in the chamber above me
The patter of little feet. . .
        —Henry Wadsworth Longfellow
        "The Children's Hour"

I'm the goddamn paterfamilias!
        —Everett McGill
        O Brother, Where Art Thou?

and to Wanda Coleman, mother of much.

ACKNOWLEDGMENTS

Thank you to the Mrs. Giles Whiting Foundation, whose generous award paid for the ιvf procedure that made much of this book possible. Deepest gratitude to Dr. Kornafel and her team, the scrc, Dr. Hill, Dr. Bochner, the staff, nurses and doctors at Good Samaritan's nicu ward, and the crew of *Deliver Me*.

Thank you to N, Tisa Bryant, CM Burroughs, LaTasha N. Nevada Diggs, Yona Harvey, Amaud Johnson, Bao Phi, Gita Sharma, and Evie Shockley for checking out and challenging drafts.

Thanks to Kate, Mark, and Red Hen Press for their constant support of my work and to the kind editors and curators of the journals, websites, and exhibitions in which versions of these poems have appeared:
Beloit Poetry Journal "Thank You But   Please Don't Buy My Children Clothes
  with Monkeys on Them"
Beyond Words: A Fusion of Poetry (+) Visual Art (+) Jazz (American Jazz Museum) "Blues Done Red"
The Economy "The Bees," "The Fly"
Fourteen Hills "Hood," "Right," "Run," "Tar," "Which"
The Iowa Review "In the End, They Were Born on tv"
The Los Angeles Review of Books "Father-to-be Takes Himself for a Walk"
miPOesias "Goooooo or Goooooo or Goooooo"
Pleiades "The Miscarriage: A List of 10 Euphemisms for Use in Stage Banter" and
  "The Miscarriage: A Minstrel Show"
Ploughshares "The Pool, 1988"
Poetry "Every Hard Rapper's Father Ever: Father of the Year," "Jim Trueblood: Father of the Year,"
  "Kronos: Father of the Year," and "Noah/Ham: Fathers of the Year"
The Rumpus "Darth Vader, King Laios (Fill Out Their Applications As, Across the Lobby,
  Genghis Khan's 'Cat's in the Cradle' Ringtone Plays): Fathers of the Year" and "Word Hunt"
SkinMag (a chapbook published by A5/Deadly Chaps, 2012) "Gator Bait"
Spiral Orb Seven "Blues Done Red"

Thanks to my family and friends, with special gratitude to Dr. Evangeline Castle, whose presence in our household was a great blessing. Thanks also to Aunt Dee, Ms. Liz, Raven, and Heidi. rip Jimmy McJamerson.

And like a driver who fractures a bone while averting a collision, I thank God.

The Los Angeles County Arts Commission, the National Endowment for the Arts, the Pasadena Arts & Culture Commission and the City of Pasadena Cultural Affairs Division, the Los Angeles Department of Cultural Affairs, the Dwight Stuart Youth Fund, and Sony Pictures Entertainment partially support Red Hen Press.

CONTENTS

IT IS DESIGNED FOR CHILDREN

GOOOOOO OR GOOOOOO OR GOOOOOO

IN THE END, THEY WERE BORN ON TV

THE POOL, 1988

Altadena-summer, mustard, smog and sun—all yellow
as I've become. for this year I fear I'm fat so I wear
a t-shirt while I swim. like a child, the t-shirt clings
to me through noons submerged in August's gut. some summers back,
I was born and breath smacked into me. this year the water
smacks me, diving yellow, round into the pool, a single
corn kernel sucked in a big blue mouth. sucked till bubbles leave
my lips and go up. I peel off the shirt, it floats then drops,
a drowned child's ghost. I let chlorine in my eyes and throat,
my cold lips hoist those first stiff hairs, masts on a murk-mouthed swell
up and on and time whipping them on whipping me surging,
something falls, this water like too much time swallowing me
all this water spitting me up and child-less as time
as history burning whip whip September whip mustache

FATHER OF THE YEAR

RAISE

to be *daddy*'s to ascend, steady, into cruelty.

a tabby bats a wren up-wise. now see
my children fall. they rise? that's fine.

no cries? great! but their arms

like chick beaks call to me. my arms
give no reply. fine. a plea strikes

some hollowed place: darlings, call that "flight."

SHAKEN

no shame in wanting to shake.
to scramble scream to sugared shush
a matter of shifting shriek
a shuffling, a shimmy.   to sleep to rest at sweet.
what you have in your hands
tears cool dark from your briquette eyes.
shuffle. shimmy.   oh baby.   shake.
                                    it won't
                              stop don't
                              stop.   you feel the beat
                oh baby.   coming on?
        no shame.
what sort of sound would it make? make you want to move?
what you have in your hands
rubs lemons in your skinned eyes."oh baby."
        shaker's sound? shake.
        you can call people!
    there are people you can call.

        calm down,
        sir. calm down,
    ma'am.   feel a beat
    no shame in wanting
                it to stop.   coming on.
    "honey, I just want you to" CALM . DOWN
        you just have to
            stop
    you just have to stop. it won't
                        stop
                        stop don't
        no shame.   "calm down!"
        they want you to call.
what you got in your hands   you shaking??????   won't
                !!!!!!!!!   "stop"don't
                            stop"don't"
                                you feel it?

THE CRICKETS

their song busts wide the family room,
hews the slim hem

between *house* and *wilds*.
I crush those bugs

to mute their tune.

EVERY HARD RAPPER'S FATHER EVER: FATHER OF THE YEAR

because we rhyme with *bother*
slant *brother, mother, smother, other*
can be slurred to *farther, author*
made of *hate, far, after, fear*
because we rhyme with *bother*
slant *brother, mother, smother, other*
can be slurred to *farther, author*
made of *hate, far, after, fear*
because we rhyme with *bother*
slant *brother, mother, smother, other*
can be slurred to *farther, author*
made of *hate, far, after, fear*
because we rhyme with *bother*
slant *brother, mother, smother, other*
can be slurred to *farther, author*
because we rhyme with *bother*
made of *hate, far, after, fear*
slant *brother, mother, smother, other*
because we rhyme with *bother*
can be slurred to *farther, author*
slant *brother, mother, smother, other*
made of *hate, far, after, fear*
because we rhyme with *bother*

and you can't you won't you don't stop
and you can't you won't you don't stop
and you can't you won't you don't stop
and you can't you won't you don't stop
and you can't you won't you don't stop
and you can't you won't you don't stop

TITUS ANDRONICUS: FATHER OF THE YEAR

TITUS
my children, bombs, but made of me.

CHORUS
a father's love, a flame.

ABRAHAM, JHVH, JOSEPH: FATHERS OF THE YEAR

I think I LOVE you. amen
amen
amen *show Me what* *you can do!*
daddy on the almighty

mountain with Daddy's Heat
across his neck. sharp stone
at his son as the Sun's
shanks go down, go his.

Daddy the Almighty   1 2 3— *stop!*
Mountain, Neck full   *you better save it!*
of sharp Heat, His Son *you better save it!*
shanked. on the Mount,
mounted. across go sun,
sun, sun: the stone gone.
never could say goodbye. . .
no! daddy the stone. full
"1, 2, 3. . ." ". . .you better—*no!*
of sharp at his sons "1, 2, 3. . ." ". . .you better *no!*
"1, 2, 3. . .". ". . . you better— *no!* almighty necks. shake,
cross, down. till the sun "1, 2, 3. . .". ". . . you better *no!*
"1, 2, 3. . ." ". . .you better *no!* go down its sharp mountain.
"1, 2, 3. . ." ". . .you better *no!*
you better *no!*
not stop! *I'll be therrrrrrrrrrrrrrrrrrrrrr*
rrrrrrrrrrrrrrrrrrrrrrrrrrrrrrrrrrrrrrrrrrrrrrrrrrrrrrrrrrrrrrr
rrrrrrrrrrrrrrrrrrrrrrrrrrrrrrr r r r rrr rr r rr rr r r r r r!!

JIM TRUEBLOOD: FATHER OF THE YEAR

there was a remember when the mama was my girl
the mama was in my girl biding to turn
my girl turn mama when what I got turn to girl
in her
my girl in my girl make my girl mama
they both mine
all three

I remember a when when I only dreamed dreams
but my dreams are remembers now
they a when

that when was when the girl I made of mama I made a mama with what I got
I tell what I tell but I know what I know
only a man make his dream a remember and ain't I a man
what's mine is mine to turn to what I dream
what I make mine to make mine
I won't 'bide what won't turn

DARTH VADER, KING LAIOS (FILL OUT THEIR APPLICATIONS AS,
ACROSS THE LOBBY, GENGHIS KHAN'S "CAT'S IN THE CRADLE"
RINGTONE PLAYS): FATHERS OF THE YEAR

FATHER OF THE YEAR

APPLICATION/SELF-NOMINATION FORM page 4 of 16

23) When was your sabre red? ONce a blue Little boy TurN black

24) What is blood to you? a Force what Force your ass To a riddle

24.a) The little boy/girl? a burst boy births his own bloody end

25) Day you died? what I did ~~nothing~~ Killed me already

26) Congratulations on becoming a father! What have you learned? I had a lot To do to dim my son

26.a) How so? To dim him was To turn him just Like me

27) Words of wisdom for him/her? iT'S nOT Shit's Fucked up That's Fucked: iT'S nOT Fucking shit up

FATHER
OF THE
YEAR

APPLICATION/SELF-NOMINATION FORM page 4 of 16

23) When was your sabre red? Once I glued the Little Boy.

24) What is blood to you? A Ripple that Ripples Ass with force.

24.a) The little boy/girl? A boy's burst end sows a bloody Birth.

25) Day you died? What I Did killed me ALREADY

26)Congratulations on becoming a father!
What have you learned? The son I cradled would get my cat.

26.a) How so? Child Arrived so much like a MAN!

27) Words of wisdom for him/her? it's NOT MotheR Fucking ; but Fucking the Motherfucking KING.

NOAH/HAM: FATHERS OF THE YEAR

two fathers are two sons and one
father prone where he's been

HEE!

HEE!

HEE!

HEE!

HEE!

and one father down a floor
is not coming up. to keep from falling:
fell. one son hits the floor, one won't
hear. one father won't open the door

HEE!

HEE!

HEE!

so one could see. to keep from failing,
one must stay prone and one can't

HEE!

HEE!

leave one down. for a son to remain father
is to level falling against keeping his son from

HEE!

HEE!

HEE!

the dark balls out the gap

of the deep blue robe—upside down islet
with a father and son's arms
to right, less wing but twig.

HEE!

HEE!

for a father to stay a son, leverage falling against failing.
that blue robe blue as a long rain.

HEE!

HEE!

two fathers, two sons, only two
can be saved. one must serve.

HEE!

the weary women in this wet house

HEE!

throw their clean hands up, cast their dry eyes down.

24

DAEDALUS: FATHER OF THE YEAR

[DAEDALUS passes his drafting desk, awash with botched schematics.]

DAEDALUS: . . .

[DAEDALUS goes through solutions to another morning's sudoku.]

DAEDALUS: . . .

[DAEDALUS flushed in loose boxers; boxed, still, the moose sheds.]

DAEDALUS: . . .

[DAEDALUS takes out his truck's old starter. his garden gone to wildrye spikes.]

DAEDALUS: . . .

[DAEDALUS reclines. the rerun's flatscreen light splashes his eyes.]

DAEDALUS: . . .

[DAEDALUS throws, again, sunflower seeds to crows.]

DAEDALUS: . . .

DADDIES! ON PLAYGROUNDS ON WEDNESDAYS

deep in soap hours lovely mothers up in our hairy wherefore wonder
what we do and why come we come and well we'll mutter
used to, gone to or *it's summer*
so the playground slide'll melt our kids to slumber puddles
that cool our hairy heads. we head off
        to not do;
        to set to;
        to wish we; Wednesday in July, muttering. lovely mothers

wonder what we do we grip sippies to our hairy nipples.
shaved hair cracks microwaved milk skin children drink drink drink to splinter!
our hairy crotches smell like jarred squash.
how we wish our toddlers found this odd
as the lovely mothers who wonder what we

do we plummet under summer sun?
our pockets at our hairy narrow hips are wing-ish.
our fathers yonder, pants jammed with floorplans, hairy balls, and wallets.
our fathers holler: "higher higher" lovely mothers, wonder what

we do we fodder that dream where *grain* means _____
and *mountains* mean _____ and _____ is the *plain?*
and you were there, and you, and you, lovely mothers.
it was but a dream and we're no hairy headshrinkers
yet don't we know what *seas* means? lovely mothers wonder

what we do, and dare inquire: our hairy nostrils whoosh
their diapers-in-the-dryer sound!
neckties flutter in our mouths
soused with answers, hairy adventures!

A B C D
1 2 3
had
sad
bad
daddies! on the playground, hell of a Wednesday
these days, burn. I used to [MUTTER. . .].
I should've. I will! this! is what we do lovely, mothers
and you?
and you?
and you?

MISCARRIAGES

SONNET DONE RED

I love your body.
I love your body.
I love your body.
I love your body.
I love your body.

I HATE IT

    o,

I love your body.
I   hate   it.

    o,

I hate
your body.

LOVE

    even so

I love your body.
  hate   it.

THE FLY

the fly's not David's down Elah-way flak;
but a quavering fleck peering at death
through fractured-up glass. still, he *flees* from it.
the boy—giant, mite—*cries* till it's killed, then
eyes avid, leers amid fingers at it.

THE MISCARRIAGE: A LIST OF 10 EUPHEMISMS FOR USE IN STAGE BANTER

foxes looted the coop!

God marked your copy!

cherries dammed the flume!

a kite fell in April!

an apple burst the nest!

some seminoles fled the field!

our wagon crashed but we just saw the heart in the furrow!

four alarm beat three days ago and next the doll factory!

roses week is Father's Day choke the cabbage!

red ants blitz the sugar bowl!

THE MISCARRIAGE: A SUNDAY FUNNY

woman
bed

woman
bed

woman
bed

woman
bed

woman
bed

woman
bed

woman
blood
bed

woman
blood
bed

woman
bed

woman
bed

woman
bed
blood

woman
blood

THE MISCARRIAGE: A MAGIC TRICK

1. stash scarlet silks in a lady's skirt.
2. plant her among the crowd.
3. call your shill to the dais.
4. lay her on your table.
5. conceal her with your bedsheet.
6. distract the crowd with patter.
7. apply a sleight between her thighs.
8. take hold the silk's loose corner.
9. pull till it pools on the floor.

PRESTO!

THE MISCARRIAGE: A SILENT FILM

to be shot without color

TITLE CARD
"Peril at Red River!"

EXT. RED RIVER 4:30 a.m.
MEDIUM SHOT
BABY in hamper rushing downriver to edge-of-frame.

EFFECTS NOTE
for BABY use sheets, wadded.

TRACKING SHOT
CAR racing the riverside.

INT. CAR
a WIFE and HUSBAND.
HUSBAND driving after BABY.
WIFE cradling her belly.

TITLE CARD
"Will They Make It in Time?"

EXT. 4:35 a.m.
LONG SHOT
waterfall, riverbed.

THE MISCARRIAGE: A MINSTREL SHOW

DAMN-NEAR DAM husband! peel your peepers of their sandgrits
imtermediately, says your beloved.

PATERFAMILISN'T I hears not a cock crow but a crow crow.
morning broke not water but tomato!

DAMN-NEAR DAM listen, my darkling. ain't I tell you not
to consummeat melon in our pallet?

PATERFAMILISN'T consummeat?

DAMN-NEAR DAM present tense of consummate.

PATERFAMILISN'T but smudgy-poo: if'n I makes to eat
sweet Georgia ham, antatomically
speaking, mustn't my palate get a piece?

DAMN-NEAR DAM lookee here, smokescreen: ain't shit aunt-tomic
bout this watermelon juice spilt betwick
and betwaint my legs. sheets to glory pinked!

PATERFAMILISN'T then I ain't red handed; you're red-gamded!
t'ain't melonade if I ain't ate any.
sides: I ain't see'ed no seeds by your fanny.

DAMN-NEAR DAM hog, hogslop and hogslop head! they making
Georgia ham seedless now. the stain's the thing!

PATERFAMILISN'T seedless!? then alas: I guess Ise undoed.

DAMN-NEAR DAM yes: un-dude. and she done. so Ise undid.
they cakewalk to the wings. ENTER, BONES.

37

THE MISCARRIAGE: A BAR JOKE

two guys walk into a bar. first guy says: "yo guy, why so down?" second guy replies: "my wife just had a miscarriage." first guy says: "I know *exactly* how you feel, I just had my girl get an abortion!"

THE MISCARRIAGE: A POETIC FORM

internal rhyme (perfect)
internal rhyme (perfect)
internal rhyme (perfect)
internal rhyme (perfect)
internal rhyme (perfect)

(volta)

internal rhyme (slant)
internal rhyme (slant)
internal rhyme (slant)

(volta)

internal rhyme (broken)

iT IS
DESIGNED
FOR
CHILDREN

WHAT IT DO DONE RED

I love your body. I hate it.

but do I hate to love your body
or do I love hating your body
or do I hate "I love your body"
or do I love your body to hate it
or do I love your body since I hate it
or do I hate loving your body because of it?

WORD HUNT

INTELLIGENT   CLEAN   PLEASANT   LOVABLE
FRIENDLY   HANDSOME   WORTHY   HONEST
INDUSTRIOUS   INNOCENT   GENEROUS   RESPECTABLE
KIND   BEAUTIFUL   GOOD   CHERISHED

```
R G E N R R G N N G G R R G G R I
N N E G E I G E R G R G E I R N E E
G G R G R N E R N E G R G E G E R N
N G E R R G R R G R I R N N R G G E
R N R E I R R G R N I R N E R N R I
G E G E R R R I E R G R E N N G R I
R N R G R N E G R E N G E R N G R
G R N G G R G R E R G N R R N R N N
R G E R R R N G G I E G R R G N R R
R G G N E E R E E I R I I G R G I E
I R N G N R I E R G E E R E R G R R
E R N G R G G R G N R G N R G N G N
G N G R N G R G R G R N G N E R N R
R G E R E N G G R N R G N R N G R N
N N G G R G E R G N E N E G R G R G
R N E R G R R N G R G R N G I I R N
```

GATOR BAIT

picaninnies been penny candies in the handbag
when it's still a-draggin in fens.

a 'dilian's grin a line of keen cones come picnicking:
"pics [HICCUP]! can't eat just one!"

gator hunger caters to being catered to;
who's slaver slakes the croc's chops?

who's so nutty for nigger toes à la cuckoo for cocoa?
who could just eat whom up?

"COSTCO PULLS 'LIL MONKEY' DOLL OFF SHELVES"—KTLA NEWS HEADLINE

THANK YOU BUT   PLEASE DON'T BUY MY CHILDREN CLOTHES
WITH MONKEYS ON THEM

see
& do WHAT IT DO say what
IT IS?

if evil
here
WHAT IT DO?
swing some into history's way.

if evil here, who hear it?
a tree fall in the rigged jungle
                    (nobody here
                      but us_____)

if evil here, who see it? WHAT
some see what sum get the get
of the once got.   (how much that lil
                            monnnkey in the window?)
if evil here, who speak it?

                DO retail re-tell the re-tailing of—
                (nobody here but us.)
    history has a way IT DO what it do.
                                    ¿

[if]   throughout history black baby bottoms's blue as a baboon's nose.

[if]   throughout history black babies get blue black bottoms till the stump
of their circumcised tails black over.

[&]   a circumcised black baby tail must not be discarded but kept
for later for show.

[thus]   a circumcised black baby's tail was often for showed
after removal in a jar or dried on the mantle
below the buck bust.

[i.f.]   sing a blues of black bottom! sing a blues of blueblack bottom!

[if]   throughout history history has a way with blueing black babies.
[or]   say history has a history of blacking black babies.
[or if] history has a history of blueblacking black babies blue.

[e.g.]   peekaboo black babies's a black mama gut bucket blues.
[i.e.]   you wanna see ma's black baby?

[&]   jigaboo black babies is history blacking over a blue black hide.

[thus]   picayune black babies's history's way
of knowing black babies is discarded
to hide its history of blacking black babies
blue as a baboon's nose knows tails.

[qed]   pitiful black-at-the-bottom-babies!

precious
lil monkeys! curlicued tails troop queries on my babies. curious
lil monkeys and the uniformed overseer—who can tame them? unruly
lil monkeys no ways tired with new IDs and bipedal reveries. musing
lil monkeys's pointless—stick them with sticks! big leaps
from their green tenements. angry
lil monkeys: go chew on the saw of "fruit-falls-when-ripe." wait! hungry
lil monkeys! smiling lil monkeys climbing pajamas.
my daughter's onesie. leering
lil monkeys pincer the cribs, bent senators,
hissing in lil monkey beards.
lil monkeys' hands all murder sopped! put your hands up!
lil monkeys shot. love for
lil monkeys?! humans over lil monkeys,
motherfucker!
lil monkeys over babies, bucking on the lamps,
messing the light, smearing
lil monkeys shadows on my son's face.
lil monkeys jibber from the nursery, porch, the street.
lil monkeys—a-ha! freeze! lil monkeys
lil monkeys foul my babies' clothes like blood, like shit.
no no
thank you no lil monkeys
noo thanks
noo o o ooo o o o
o o o

a ha
a
h
a
h !!
!

black babies's born fit with looney tune gloves
        over fists a-bristling opposable thumbs.
black babies in monkeysuits's nude as birds;
        save onionskin sheets on their genital bunches.
black babies's genitals learn to sign quickly—
        they do what they see and they don't stop no show.
black babies's last seen as blacker than not
        and they can't stay getting away with it.
black babies's found up in trees and on sidewalks.
        we fetch them with dust-bins and mops when it's done.

HOOD

the curbstone breaking the woods while
the wolf in cottage light. in a hood, the child.

there're teethful queries at doing what
and to where. in felt cap, the wolf,

or the hunter wear the pelt. if felled would
no one but the mother hear the child.

limbs scrabbling at dim streetlamps. as rife as all out,
the wolf-haired gut gorge and get kill-fatted.

still, the good good villagers sleep like clean hatchets.

there is something vaguely sadistic about many fables—those that seek to instruct children,
by means of fear. —Carl Phillips

WHICH

was it he who unlatched him at, then afoul,
night's face? ate up what trace he crumbled?

had to have lost himself in adrenaline's hard cake
and his eyes like ovens. someone, cackling,

out a cage and in, fixing for to slip
that slim bone jive to believe it alive.

wrestled him to eager heat once he pry
the lock he locked. all through somebody's

copse he shadow his shadow's nothing body.

two new narratives are set into motion—the narratives of our distance from
and approximation to the mythic. —Carl Phillips

RUN

cooked up a sharp sweet someone
set to get bit then out the kitchen

into the sorrowful always of trees like trouser
legs as if grass-stained but just a figure

of speech *hahahaha* some body sprint
gingerly between dusk's wan pants run

hot through the telling carry someone
in someone's sly mouth and done

at the story's reddest place.

*fable—especially in the context of the fairy tale. . . becomes a means of pointing out
the dangers of empiricism. more often than not, it is designed for children.* —Carl Phillips

RIGHT

beasts in the manor, babe in the firs so nothing fit
but the tale gone to burn each loose lip

or like the story on the tongue too cold
won't sit right. lie down into it, what's said

turn from what got broke, tossing out
something hard, soft for what sound just

right there, *that's* the one. under the old yarn's cover,
one must sleep through the footsteps what whisper:

"this isn't where *you're* meant to" then them claws.

*part of the appeal of myth and fable is that these archetypal stories are and are not
our stories.* —Carl Phillips

TAR

by the roadside, rude and odd and who
is it? won't it speak when it know better to?

every wrong word caught in its dumb trap
and how dare it think it is? the hit happen

next, as if to say to dull darkness: *hey.*
here I am being here so *hey. hey!*

*HEY*gone. and still by the roadside,
stuck, presence in to absence spattered

in that black ever mess.

*we give flesh to word, and in that sense are custodians of myth, responsible not just
for the fact of its survival but for how—in what version—it will survive.* —Carl Phillips

THE BEES

because terrorizing, terror are praxes,
the twins take turns at the plush bug proxy.
the one harries
the other; from the one,
the other scurries;
bee bee! each screeches.

too sweet trees buzz, the morning blanching.

GOOOooO
OR
GOOOOOOO
OR
GOOOOOOO

SENTENCE DONE RED

I love your body. I hate it.

you think *and* *how can* *sometimes* *but* *since*

I love your body. I hate it.

choose *and* your body in my teeth like tongue, meat,
if *you think* I bite your tongue and say "my blood"
or *how can* I want the why of the way but for what
maybe *sometimes* my marshmallow teeth vs. my brick tongue
but my tongue a bag at my teeth's red door, weeeeell,
though *since* a mouth is a hole and so yours and all teeth are mine
making voids in meat.

GOOOOOO OR GOOOOOO OR GOOOOOO

seeds, or chris rock says keep her off the pole
here is a truth about pornography (#5):
good for goo getting but the comes-
back-around bristles stiffen when——

oooo
baby baby-making *with* your baby in the family way
a——deed deed deed——

solo sorties into the sordid sort of seem——men like what
they like like what they——

for me   I   like some stranger's daughter
——what if——
oh   baby——when I cum   think *wife*
a——word word word——

GOD we cry
the *oooo*
baby is prayer wish——

what's this? who's that?
an address? a pet?

will baby take after the mother——
or someone's open daughter——
babies' lives in my palm——real life
——stiffen——
petroleum goo goes to plastic–jar

stripper-heel-clear
–falls from the pole

traffic jam and jar of semen
no where for a brake squeal of moments and still there   my still car
hauling the Valley behind   car before me lugging me hauling
the Valley and the car before dragging the lugging and hauling   Russian
dollish we all inside the hour cars rush and inside the hour
our cars still   car I'm inside with what was inside me outside now
but inside the jar here in the car——*goooooo* the hour burns down
in brake lights and what I had in me hasn't hours out——
goooooo caroms in the car   go go go go burst quarter notes at
the windows I roll down——dying out there on all that air

staring then wwssssh!
DOC K bids me witness my excess *goo goo* goo polliwogging
below the lens   end is nigh for panicked Left Behinds
of the baster Rapture   trapped on a flat glass slide
eyeless staring squiggles   the microscope sky   Dad's dark pupil agog

wooooow

and DOC K knows a blow job joke

"was it   yes   Woody Allen's"   DOC and I yuk
enter N   I say: "you gotta see this   c(C)reation!"   the blind
fry of the hidden sea   we stare and stare until starried
we leave   the DOC——goddess   atheist——at the sink

OHSS and how the uterus resembles a bull's skull

DOC said mom-to-be will tote stones in her a week-or-so
bangles dangling from the horns of her inner steer   N a Hera
-kles wrassling the cattle-headed pebble-vexed beast to work

                    under night and over flesh I rub her buried toro
playing Deianeira fondling a half-goddish thew   I coo
oh baby   my only language for what's being done

when "oh" N ohs when "oh" the stones
  pelt the spooked bull rattles the pen
"oh!" no "oh!" all night we googly-eyed expecting
  to spot red

baby named, booked

baby(not yet) ambulates the bull skull
of mommy's(not yet) sex   in the pocket   the cut
creeping deep-end diver grows(we hope) in the drown   expat
of daddy's(not yet) groin with dual citizenship
and not yet missy nor mister   mariney nor tar
civílly nor banger   sissy nor breeder   the future?   "nigger"
ain't maybe gaveled in *that* muscly court   the judge(s) out
so the parents(not yet) bite red they lips' rinds
front-rowed and walleyed in Sunday duds   jury by and by
and bailiff(ever) locked loaded goon   entrance
and parents(not yet) wail *baby? baby?* here come de—

curious sex as tauromachy as sex

Friday night   we want to make   make want
on a couch with a bed in its paunch
what-we-want is about
inside the bull skull   my My asks:
what's in it?   what's in it?
her Her:
don't know come check
inside
what's in it? what's in it?
don't know
come check
inside it   ropas on the floor
flores on the plaza
what's in it? what's in
it?   don't know   come check
seeds; no stone?
picador I pick one
                    seeds
                    not stone
bullpen sprung open
begs: *toro toro*
no flores like sangre
we go into good singing
                    taking-turns-at-prayer
                    taking-turns-at-hothouse altars
o baby   we do we do
what's in it?   what's in it?
don't know come check

       take prayers in
                      in our hips' wet break
in it   night on something
what's in it? what's in it?
something in it on the air
don't know come check   the room
full of *baby o*
      baby
what's in it? what's in it?
don't know come check
       poor matadora/¿toro?
          ¿toro?
            we don't know no no
            her panties turning muleta
            sangre flowers up the plaza's dust

tuesday morning at work

she calls her back an ache. and knowing blood means no
baby no I know the cellphone's a wound of words *baby no.*
only language. *so sorry. I lo—*
but it's off. the cut shut
in her purse. my tinny words. she goes
to bleed on the toilet.
this ain't shit. this ain't. shut
the stall's a broken room.

know there's nothing now to lose.
in her purse: my *gonna*
be ok baby oh. call me. . . trembles.
nothing to lose
except her body's oldest argument.
accept a stop sign in the cotton. unmentionable.
blood means no blood. that's what.
she quits the stall and says nothing. this is work
I don't know. soon we'll roll that stone again maybe.
for now *no baby oh* in her pocketbook
I'm so sorry for now
stop.

THE LADYBUGS

hundreds knife the lawn and maul the sky.
the tyke shrieks, red red red reds his eyes.

OUT MY HANDS

just because I'm jerking off don't mean I don't want babies.
the doctor's coat is panty white—here, nothing's clean as panties.
I don't know where she takes my wife but surely there's a mattress;
I'm hunkered in the men's room watching someone get sucked off,
wishing someone'd bend another over something.

this spit of mine's too filthy and could kill these kids-to-be
so I stroke bone dry to fill the sterile cup.
it's days before the smut flakes off my cock. but so what?

when a curtain and a surgeon saw a furrow into N,
there've been seven months of hurling for her waist to turn vagina.

that's some woman you got there, boy.

IN THE
END,
THEY'
WERE
BORN
ON TV

BLUES DONE RED

‖:I love your body. I hate it. :‖}———

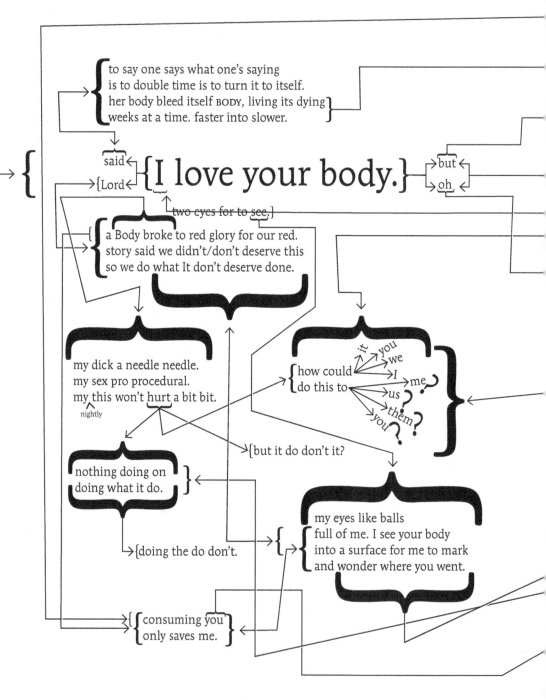

to say one says what one's saying
is to double time is to turn it to itself.
her body bleed itself BODY, living its dying
weeks at a time. faster into slower.

said
{Lord

{I love your body.}

but
oh

two eyes for to see.}

a Body broke to red glory for our red.
story said we didn't/don't deserve this
so we do what It don't deserve done.

my dick a needle needle.
my sex pro procedural.
my this won't hurt a bit bit.
nightly

how could
do this to
it
you
we
I
me
us
them
you

{but it do don't it?

nothing doing on
doing what it do.

{doing the do don't.

my eyes like balls
full of me. I see your body
into a surface for me to mark
and wonder where you went.

{consuming you
only saves me.

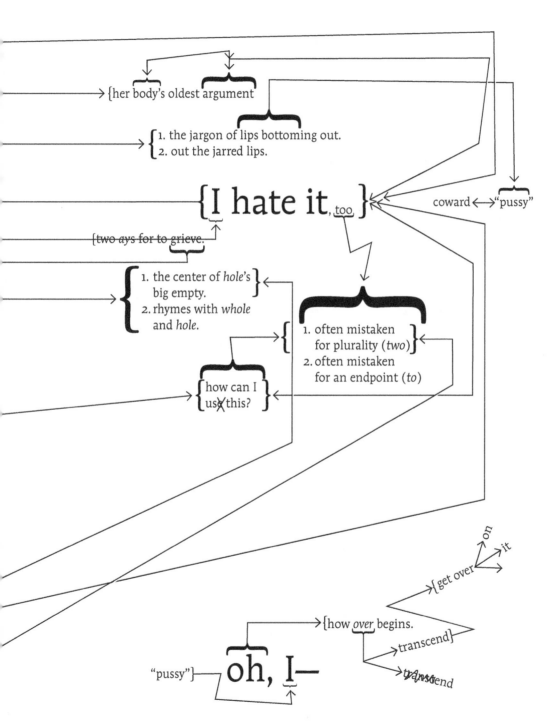

{her body's oldest argument

1. the jargon of lips bottoming out.
2. out the jarred lips.

{I hate it, too }← coward ←→ "pussy"

~~{two *ays* for to grieve.~~

1. the center of *hole's* big empty.
2. rhymes with *whole* and *hole*.

1. often mistaken for plurality (*two*)
2. often mistaken for an endpoint (*to*)

{how can I use this?

{get over ← on → it

{how *over* begins.

→ transcend}

→ ~~transcend~~

"pussy"} oh, I—

"...IN DEEP WATER / WHO..."—YONA HARVEY

HOLD

it's a squall world and newly round. your body
hijacked and what a waterful hull.
them nigh people in the hold drum *gruel!*
gruel! you pump sump and sea heaves-to, mutineers
jury-rigging your rigging till taking on, you founder,
warping like oaken plank in dank ocean.

KRONOS: FATHER OF THE YEAR

my mouth a cunt in reverse and my guts, nuts.
I nose the hushed nursery, belly for my dick spurting ink at shit.

Fire. Darkness.
Water. Harvest.
you know no kid's name a word, but some shit-to-do.
no kid ain't shit but a map to its folk
traced by its folk to where they buried their folk.

took that shit that made me to make me make myself myself,
rolled in on papa's red nuts like they a fucking chariot.

                    ...

these days my guts stay aching. my head an empty crib.

I sit to my work on me to work on. life is its own hunger for itself.
I want only one to feed.

FATHER-TO-BE TAKES HIMSELF FOR A WALK

out!
the final hospital stay's a leash,
so I'm bound to the bed N lay a week in,
weak to the *beep* of her flashflood blood
run these mudslide years of red.
I scratch at the window like some mutt
the night before strangers dump the trash.

N's a shotgun aimed at us.

come dawn, her doctor pulls her trigger,
bucks me into *Father.*
my stomach guards my wilting cock,
snarls at trespassing clocks.
N gnaws her steepled fingers.
I leave her there for food.

beg!
a fucked week sick with Korean burritos:
half-breed comida muk-da'ing my withering wallet.
that food truck chuckles to the hospital's lot,
"his parking stubs *stay* at daily max!"

damn I am tonight too mutt
for kalbi, kimchee, tomatillo,
I'm full of what I don't comprendo—
but dusk's a bloody chuck patty on the greasy griddle sky.
the stars: they sizzle. they pop.

heel!
walking west 6ᵀᴴ my shadow shies from MacArthur Park's heat and shivs.
not me though!
these new mongrel senses
are open wounds among lemon-tinted storefronts.

but what's it to know when today come yesterday
I'll no longer not be a father?
so long as tomorrow is tomorrow
        and yesterday's yesterday
                stays nearer to the bloody years of not knowing—
        yet I'm not long for what I've been so long
and so near to what I'm going to,
        tonight I am just a man and not quite
                a father so nearly not just a man
        and so?

babbling shopglass of bright ads, my reflection halved,
all I can't read as I pass.

down!
my eyes sic the bustling Food 4 Less.
my pissant shadow rank as a cur's piss.
I pack no pistol, speak no Spanish:
what future? unborn names sud my black-ass lips,
my heart a red dick out my head's hairy sheath.
my own dick abuts my haunch.
somebody put me down!

down a side street:
overgrown terraces calamitous with foreignness.

swearing the curbed cars are explosions
fixing to be cut out themselves, I'm down
the street's dividing line, my nose busted
with cumin, menudos, cinnamon.

>   *speak!*
I die at dawn, so I set to prowl
the mongrel hours God's silvered eye
hounds fools and children. stupid, childish
man's heart pump no Kool Aid, though!
I bark at near dark: *who wants some?!*
I could upchuck my lupine alarm at sudden blood.

but with sun comes soon some new tether to hitch my throat
and stifle now knee even now pants now
shook and up now stand now
dawn now these dull teeth
say the names, boy. speak!

THE PILLBUG

like a toy with that stupid nickname
and you aren't stupid, lil' lady,
so you oughtn't call it "roly-poly,"
right? daughter, call it "sowbug":
it can't turn against itself when it's afraid.
don't be stupid, lil' lady. s-o-w-

HOME SHOWS

belly swollen, overrun, N regards those crumbling homes.
each TV dawn, their owners groan: *we didn't know—*.

then, MAN hammers holes in cellar walls,
while WOMAN boots loose window sills.
who did this wiring tuts HARD HAT's yellow shell
at a nest of knots and copper coils.
this plumbing's a mess of running rust.
all's awry behind the paint's smooth face.

N pukes blank juices, flushes her tubes with saline.
fading, waking as each ruin tumbles into another.

"I want to see the end," she mumbles—
half in dream—when pick-ups gallop across the sod,
tools gleam in gutted rooms,
expectant houses beam . . . *like new!* . . . *like new!*

IN THE END, THEY WERE BORN ON TV

i. good reality TV
a couple wanted to be -to-be and TV wants the couple-to-be
to be on TV. the people from TV believe we'd be good TV
because we had wanted to be to-be and failed and now might.

to be good at TV make-like TV isn't. make-like living in our living room
and the TV crew isn't there and the boom isn't there
saving the woman from TV's voice that won't be there
saying *tell us about the miscarriage.* in the teeming evening
and some dog barking at all we cannot hear.

ii. would you be willing to be on TV?
people in their house on TV are ghosts haunting a house haunting houses.
pregnant women in their houses on TV are haunted houses haunting a house
    haunting houses.
our living room a set set for us ghosts to tell ghost stories on us.

would you be to-be on TV?
to be the we we weren't to be and the we we're-to-be to be on TV.
the pregnant woman agrees to being a haunted house
haunting flickering houses. yes ok yeah yes.

iii. forms
in the waiting room for the doctor to TV the pregnant woman's insides
out on a little TV on TV. filling a form on TV is to flesh into words
on a sheet that fills up with you. yes yes and turn to the receptionist
only to turn back to a ghost waiting to be officially haunted yes.

a magazine riffles itself on TV; loud pages, a startled parrot
calls your name then alighting on magazines

and waddle the hall you -to-be and the TV crew that isn't going to be there
on TV and the doctor and you are looking at her little TV on TV the doctor
says *see? there they are.* ghosts sound themselves out to flicker on the little TV.
there they go to the pregnant woman scared to be such good TV.

iv. cut
to one-more-time-from-the-top yourself
is to ta-daaaaa breathing. the curtain drops, plush guillotine.
would you talk about the miscarriage one more time? ta-daaaaa

v. all the little people out there
after she was a haunted house before we haunted us for TV then
the pregnant woman watched TV. vomit on her teeth like sequins.

our TV stayed pregnant with the people from TV's TV show
pregnant with haunted houses wailing then smiling up into our living room.

it helps she said of the people from TV's TV show so *yes* then to TV to help,
she said, the haunted houses in the living rooms we said *yes* to help
thousands of wailing houses.

vi. only with some effort
the best ghosts trust they're not dead. no
no the best ghosts don't know how not to be alive.
like being good at TV.

inside the pregnant woman, the -to-be of the family-who-failed-
but-now-might-be-to-be were good TV.
but the we-who-failed butterfingered and stuttered,
held our hands like we just got them.

we've been trying so long we said *we can't believe it this is finally happening.*

vii. scheduled c-section: reality TV
and they're born made of meats on TV!
the doctor voilàs them from the woman's red guts
into the little punch bowls.

the new mother says *I want to see them my babies!*

the doctor shoves the new mother's guts back, express lane grocer.

the demure camera good TVs up two meat babies into wailing ghosts.

off, the new mother's blood like spilled nail polish.

viii. ghost story
did you know about dogs and ghosts? one barking at one's nothing?

ix. the miscarriage: exposition for reality TV
it helps to be on TV. we want to be good on TV. ok yes.
to help we want to be good TV. yeah yes.
please tell me about the miscarriage.

the woman from TV wants good TV and *something specific that gets you right*
in the tear to the eye to milk the pregnant woman's breasts heavy with—.

good, we talk about the dead one on TV.

it was horrible, the blood was everywhere that morning a dog barks.
one-more-time-from-the-top. *it was horrible, the blood was everywherrrrr*
doggone dog goes on. on to take three and *it was horri*BOOM
in the boom goes the barking and bad TV! bad TV! we want to help
being good TV *please tell me about the miscarriage*
one more time *it was*

x. after the c-section was more like
the doctor shoving the new mother's guts in, jilted lover packing a duffel.

xi. talking about the miscarriage: behind the scenes
please tell me about the miscarriage
please tell me about the miscarriage
please tell me about the miscarriage
please tell me about the miscarriage
the fifth take and *it was horrible,* that's all.
they call them takes, again we're robbed.

xii.
did it help watching a house fill with haunting every room
or help haunting the house? watch! here we are:
an expanding family of ghosts. we aren't here but yes ok yeah yes.
did it help? and even now know yes they were born on TV
but before *it was horrible* wasn't it must have been. please tell me
about the miscarriage for I don't know how not to be telling
and the dog growls still and still and still

FOR E.S.K.

HEIRLOOM

the windstorm's strewn shit mars the yard,
we're two dawns pitched in the blackout since.

my boy's diapered groin's wet as blueberries
and winter's crow foot skritches there.

know I did what I should in changing him
but was it black-blue quills or I goaded
that welted moan strung up his fretted throat?
the hand-me-down sound's not mine, but ante-jook juju—
blues me to his *patteroll'*, *Parchman*, *manacle*.

the boy's eyeballs clench, then turn me loose,
glare toward our sliding door:
scourged air, wrenched trees, the turd-dark dirt,
and roots upturned, asunder.

FOR K.E.K.

"I HAVE A PENIS! MAMA HAS A PENIS!"

a song in me of my daughter's wayward penis,
twin to her brother's stolid one. gone
on its hero's wanderings, audacious penis!

it's nautical, my daughter's penis,
a craft of sail, propeller, or oar,
madcap ship of the frothy bath sea penis!

it's chthonic, my daughter's penis,
unseen mine car of the dank dydee ore,
in the brimstone stony shit caves deep penis!

twin to her brother's staid one, her sly penis
sways like wry rye down by a briarpatch, brown
cackling rabbit penis. *my penis,*

my penis! she shouts, grinning at her denim,
the wee shorts's waistband's pink bow knotting
a nothing finger: REMEMBER YOUR PENIS penis!

like a balding friar, I murmur VAGINA! VAGINA!
the v's open scissor, the A's snipped shut.
but her impossible hydra penis sprouts
anew two at a time! rockets to the front
like fighter jets, Chief Master Sergeant penis!

I have a penis! mama has a penis!
she hollers. how her penis colonizes
and occupies! conqueror, liberator penis!

I teeter at her swelling ranks
and slip upon the blood slick wake
panting VAGINA... VAGINA...
the word, red with cockamamie menace.
my tongue, red as a teacher's pen is.

THE ANTS

you might think might drives the child's thumb
to grind the ant line to the pavement.

that she tries on cruelty like her daddy's hat;
it sinks over her eyes. perhaps.

but she ham-hands a crayon after, see its paths
as she jabs it, haphazard in the tablet, a shambles.

NEW PARENTS

pick through your blood but you won't find
what must be done with the others,
the ones in ice where you belong.

choosing worries you in its mouths:
lose them to strange names and houses,
board them ever in dear freezers,
or let them thaw and spoil?

those you've chosen doze under wool.
think of all the nights cool siblings
take them hand-in-hand and lead them
down the bleak rounds to your judgment.

and when their cries rise through night's slab,
driving you, beset, against their cribs,
do they grieve for those whom they have lost
or what they must have:
your eyes burnt with love,
your teeth keen on silence?

NOTES

"Abraham, JHVH, Joseph: Fathers of the Year" uses lyrics from "ABC," composed by Alphonso Mizell, Berry Gordy, Jr., Deke Richards, and Freddie Perren; "The Love You Save," composed by The Corporation; "Never Can Say Goodbye," composed by Clifton Davis; and "I'll Be There," composed by Berry Gordy, Jr., Bob West, Hal Davis, and Willie Hutch.

"Jim Trueblood: Father of the Year" features Jim Trueblood from Ralph Ellison's *Invisible Man*.

"Darth Vader, King Laios (Fill Out Their Applications As, Across the Lobby, Genghis Khan's 'Cat's in the Cradle' Ringtone Plays): Fathers of the Year" interpolates lyrics from "Cat's in the Cradle," composed by Harry Chapin. The role of Vader was played by Mike Bryant.

"Daddies! On the Playground on Wednesdays" interpolates lines from Dr. Seuss's *Hop on Pop*, originally published by Random House in 1963.

"The Miscarriage: A Sunday Funny" was inspired by Lillian-Yvonne Bertram's "The Science of Heart" from *But A Storm Is Blowing from Paradise*, chosen by Claudia Rankine as winner of the 2010 Benjamin Saltman Award, published by Red Hen Press in 2012.

"Gator Bait" was inspired by the work of Kyla Wazana Tompkins and Harryette Mullen.

"Hood," "Which," "Run," "Right," and "Tar" each feature a quotation from Carl Phillips's essay, "Myth and Fable: Their Place in Poetry," as published in *Coin of the Realm*, Graywolf Press, Saint Paul, MN 2004.

"Hold" was inspired by Yona Harvey's "Sound—Part 2: Hearing My Daughter's Heartbeat the First Time" from *Hemming the Water,* Four Way Books, Tribeca, NY 2013.

"'I Have a Penis! Mama Has a Penis!'" quotes K.E.K. and was stylistically inspired by Brendan Constantine.

ABOUT THE AUTHOR

Poet/performer/librettist Douglas Kearney's first full-length collection
of poems, *Fear, Some*, was published in 2006 by Red Hen Press. His second,
The Black Automaton (Fence Books, 2009), was Catherine Wagner's selection
for the National Poetry Series. It was also a Pen Center USA Award finalist
in 2010. That same year, Corollary Press released his chapbook-as-broadsides-
as-LP, *Quantum Spit*. His newest chapbook is *SkinMag* (A5/Deadly Chaps, 2012).
He has received a Whiting Writers Award, a Coat Hanger award and fellowships
at Idyllwild and Cave Canem. Raised in Altadena, CA, he lives with his family
in California's Santa Clarita Valley. He teaches at CalArts.